DATE DUE

NOV 2 7 2004		
MAR 2 6 2005		
MAY 0 5 2005		
MAY 3 1 2005		
NOV 2 6 2005		

DEMCO 38-296

SIMPLY SCIENCE

Plants

by Melissa Stewart

Content Adviser: Fred R. Barrie,
Visiting Assistant Curator, Field Museum of Natural History, Chicago, Illinois

Science Adviser: Terrence E. Young Jr., M.Ed., M.L.S.,
Jefferson Parish (La.) Public Schools

Reading Adviser: Dr. Linda D. Labbo,
Department of Reading Education, College of Education,
The University of Georgia

 COMPASS POINT BOOKS
Minneapolis, Minnesota

Compass Point Books
3109 West 50th Street, #115
Minneapolis, MN 55410

Visit Compass Point Books on the Internet at *www.compasspointbooks.com*
or e-mail your request to *custserv@compasspointbooks.com*

Photographs ©: PhotoDisc, cover, 7, 27; Milton Rand/Tom Stack & Associates, 4; Tom & Therisa
Stack/Tom Stack & Associates, 5; DigitalVision, 6, 23; Index Stock Imagery, 8, 12, 13, 18, 20;
Steve McCutcheon/Visuals Unlimited, 9; Michael Boys/Corbis, 10; David Aubrey/Corbis, 11;
Brand X Pictures, 14, 28; Carol Fuegi/Corbis, 15; Comstock, 16, 17; Skjold Photographs, 19;
Gay Bumgarner/Visuals Unlimited, 21; Tom Brakefield/Corbis, 24.

Editors: E. Russell Primm, Emily J. Dolbear, and Catherine Neitge
Photo Researchers: Svetlana Zhurkina and Marcie Spence
Photo Selector: Linda S. Koutris
Designer/Page Production: Bradfordesign, Inc./Erin Scott, SARIN creative

Library of Congress Cataloging-in-Publication Data
Stewart, Melissa.
  Plants / by Melissa Stewart.
     p. cm. — (Simply science)
 Summary: Briefly describes the plant structures, photosynthesis, life cycles and discusses the
importance of plants to animals and humans.
 Includes bibliographical references
   ISBN 0-7565-0444-9 (hardcover)
   1. Plants—Juvenile literature. 2. Botany—Juvenile literature. [1. Plants. 2. Ecology.] I. Title.
II. Simply science (Minneapolis, Minn.)
   QK49 .S748 2003
   580—dc21   2002010060

Table of Contents

*Note: In this book, words that are defined in the glossary are
in **bold** the first time they appear in the text.*

How are spongy mosses in a swamp and tall redwood trees in a forest alike? How is the duckweed on a pond like the mucuna vines that hang from trees? Mosses, redwoods, duckweed, and mucunas are all plants.

More than 275,000 different kinds of plants live on Earth. They can be found all over the planet. They are in fields and forests, in oceans, and on

◀ Whether it's moss near the ground or a very tall tree, plants have certain traits in common.

Vines are plants, too. ▶

mountains. They live in lakes and deserts. Some can even live in Earth's coldest places. Some plants live just a few months. Others keep growing for thousands of years. Not all kinds of plants grow in all parts of the world.

The first plants lived on land about 450 million years ago. **Fossils** tell us that the first land plants were like mosses.

Joshua trees can grow only in the desert.

Plants are found in many different places and come in several shapes and sizes. ▶

They had to live in moist places. The first plants with flowers lived 135 million to 140 million years ago. Most of the plants alive today are related to these early flowering plants.

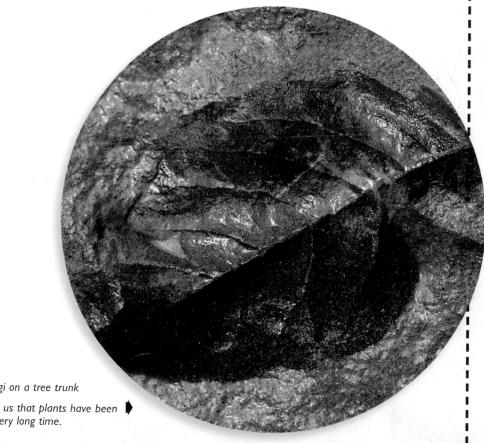

◀ Moss and fungi on a tree trunk

Leaf fossils tell us that plants have been ▶
around for a very long time.

Roots, Stems, and Leaves

Most plants have roots, stems, and leaves. A plant's roots hold it in place in the ground. Roots also absorb, or take in, water and **minerals** from the soil. A plant cannot grow without water and minerals. The roots of some plants store food.

A plant's stem gives it support. Tubes in the stems of most plants carry water and minerals from the roots

The roots of parsnip plants store food.

The roots of this plant help it get water and minerals from the soil.

to the leaves. Another set of tubes moves food through the plant.

All plants make their own food. When sunlight hits the leaves of a plant, photosynthesis takes place. Photosynthesis is the way plants make food. During photosynthesis, energy from the sun, **carbon dioxide** from the air, and water combine to form sugar. Photosynthesis also makes the oxygen you breathe.

◀ Tubes in this flower's stem carry food, water, and minerals.

When sunlight hits these leaves, ▶ photosynthesis occurs.

Plant leaves come in many different sizes and shapes. Maple trees have large, wide leaves. This is important because these trees often live in shady forests. The big leaves help maples collect all the sun energy they need. Cacti live in hot, dry deserts. They have thin, sharp spines. The spines protect cacti from enemies. Maple trees and cacti are made in ways that

◀ *Cactus spines help protect the plant.*
A maple tree has big leaves. ▶

help them grow in their **habitats**. A maple tree would dry up and die in a desert. A cactus could never live in a cool, shady forest. The kind of plants found in a habitat depends on the place's temperature and the amount of water it gets. The kind of soil is also important.

Pine trees do better in a cold, snowy environment.

A dry climate is a good place for desert plants to grow.

Plants to Seeds to Plants

A plant uses the food it makes during photosynthesis to grow. Many plants also use food energy to make beautiful flowers. When flowers bloom, they attract bees, butterflies, and other insects. These insects sip the sugary nectar that a plant makes and stores inside its flowers. The insects also pick up bits of pollen. When a bee moves to a new flower, some of

Colorful flowers will attract insects, such as butterflies, which enjoy the sweet nectar.

Plants and Animals

The plants and animals living in a habitat depend on each other. Many plants depend on insects to move pollen. Birds and other animals help plants by carrying their seeds to new places.

Animals need plants, too. Many animals make their homes in or near plants. Many insects, birds, and larger creatures eat plant leaves, stems, flowers, and fruits. Plants are at the bottom of almost every **food chain** on Earth.

During photosynthesis, a plant makes its own food. A plant uses some

Many animals, such as ▶ this panda, eat plants.

of its food energy to live and grow. It stores the rest in its roots, stems, and leaves. When a rabbit eats grass, some of the plant's stored energy passes into the animal's body. When a fox eats the rabbit, the fox uses some of the energy to live and grow.

When the fox dies, its body becomes food for **bacteria** and **fungi** that live in the soil. As these tiny creatures break down the fox's body, they release minerals into the ground. The plants that take in these minerals grow big and strong. They make better food for rabbits and cows and people.

◀ *If the fox catches and eats this rabbit, energy will pass from the rabbit to the fox.*

People and Plants

Like rabbits and cows, humans are animals that eat plants. Heads of lettuce are the leaves of plants. Celery stalks are the stems of another plant. Apples and oranges are fruit. Peas are seeds. Even bread, pasta, and chocolate chip cookies are made from plants. You would not have a strong, healthy body if you did not eat plants.

Plants give much more than just food. Cotton T-shirts are made from plants. So are paper, pencils, and many medicines. Some homes are built from wood. Some people burn wood to heat

A cow depends on plants to survive. ▶

their homes. Plants keep land from washing away during heavy rainstorms. They also make the oxygen you breathe.

You could not live in a world without plants. That is why it is so important to protect the places where plants grow.

◀ *These children are learning how wood is used to build new homes.*

Glossary

bacteria—tiny living things

carbon dioxide—a gas that is a mixture of carbon and oxygen; it has no color or odor; people and animals breathe carbon dioxide out, while plants take it in during the day

digestive system—the part of an animal's body that breaks down food; your digestive system includes your mouth, stomach, and intestines

food chain—the living things through which energy passes as one animal eats the next

fossils—the remains of plants or animals that lived long ago

fungi—living things that are neither plants nor animals; fungi feed on rotting things in the soil

habitat—places where plants or animals live

minerals—natural solid materials that are not alive

Did You Know?

• Some plants do not grow in soil. They get all the food they need from the air and water. The roots of duckweed hang a few inches below the surface of still ponds and lakes. Spanish moss and orchids are air plants. They hang from the branches of tall trees.

Want to Know More?

At the Library

Burnie, David. *Plant*. New York: Dorling Kindersley, 2000.

Chapman, Andrew. *I Wonder Why Trees Have Leaves: And Other Questions About Plants*.
   New York: Kingfisher, 1997.

Hewitt, Sally. *Plants and Flowers*. Danbury, Conn.: Children's Press, 1999.

On the Web

The Science Explorer

http://www.exploratorium.edu/science_explorer/index.html

For fun hands-on activities and experiments about all kinds of science subjects

Aggie Horticulture Just for Kids

http://aggie-horticulture.tamu.edu/kindergarden/index.html

For an introduction to the many ways children can interact with plants and the outdoors

Through the Mail

National Agricultural Library

10301 Baltimore Avenue

Beltsville, MD 20705

301/504-5755

To write for more information about growing plants for food

On the Road

Brooklyn Botanic Garden

1000 Washington Avenue

Brooklyn, NY 11225

718/623-7200

To see more than 12,000 kinds of plants from around the world

Index

About the Author

Melissa Stewart earned a bachelor's degree in biology from Union College and a master's degree in science and environmental journalism from New York University. She has written more than thirty books for children and has contributed articles to a variety of magazines for adults and children. In her free time, Melissa enjoys hiking and canoeing near her home in Marlborough, Massachusetts.